Student User Guide for

Psychology

PsykTrek 3.0

Enhanced 5th Edition

James S. Nairne
Purdue University

Prepared by Wadsworth | Cengage Learning

WADSWORTH
CENGAGE Learning™

Australia • Brazil • Japan • Korea • Mexico • Singapore • Spain • United Kingdom • United States

WADSWORTH
CENGAGE Learning™

Student User Guide for Psychology PsykTrek 3.0 Enhanced
Fifth Edition
James S. Nairne

Publisher: Linda Schreiber

Editor: Jon-David Hague

Assistant Editor: Trina Tom

Editorial Assistant: Kelly Miller

Marketing Manager: Elisabeth Rhoden

Marketing Communications Manager: Talia Wise

Project Manager, Editorial Production: Holly Rudelitsch

Creative Director: Rob Hugel

Art Director: Vernon Boes

Print Buyer: Rebecca Cross

Permissions Editor: Bob Kauser

Production Service: Elm Street Publishing Services

Text Designer: Lisa Henry

Photo Researcher: Bill Smith Group

Copy Editor: Sara Black

Cover Designer: Denise Davidson

Cover Image: Robert Llewellyn/zefa/Corbis

Compositor: Integra Software Services Pvt. Ltd.

Photo Credits: Page 11: A monster of an illusion, explaining Ponzo illusion. Ponzo illustration from *Mind Sights* by Roger N. Shepard, © 1990 by Roger N. Shepard. Reprinted by permission of Henry Holt & Co., LLC.; Page 12: Wadsworth Collection; Page 16: Archives of the History of American Psychology, University of Akron, Akron, Ohio; Page 34: © Yousuf Karsh/Hans Selye/Woodfin Camp & Associates

ISBN-13: 978-0-8400-3309-3
ISBN-10: 0-8400-3309-5

Wadsworth
20 Davis Drive
Belmont, CA 94002-3098
USA

Cengage Learning is a leading provider of customized learning solutions with office locations around the globe, including Singapore, the United Kingdom, Australia, Mexico, Brazil, and Japan. Locate your local office at **www.cengage.com/global**

Cengage Learning products are represented in Canada by Nelson Education, Ltd.

To learn more about Wadsworth, visit **www.cengage.com/wadsworth**

Purchase any of our products at your local college store or at our preferred online store **www.ichapters.com**

Printed in Canada
1 2 3 4 5 6 7 13 12 11 10 09

INTRODUCTION

Included in this Student User Guide are eighteen PsykTrek 3.0 Modules that identify some of the most enduring topics to understand in psychology. As a preview to the modules, read the "What's It For?" feature for an overview of the topic, the "Psychology For a Reason" feature, which highlights major concepts and terms, and "Practical Solutions," which provides real-world examples that apply these major concepts to life outside the classroom.

Instructions

1. Open the card you received with this booklet for login instructions and access code.
2. After registering your code, make sure you turn off your popup blocker and click the link for "Weiten's PsykTrek 3.0. . ." to access CengageNOW.
3. Select "Study Tools" and click on the PsykTrek cover to access the Table of Contents and begin using PsykTrek. Note that videos do not appear until the narrator has finished talking.
4. **Important:** When you take a quiz/test from "Study Tools," it will not show up in the gradebook. To make sure your quiz results make it into the gradebook, click "Assignment" to view the assignments your instructor has created for the course. Simulations are graded "taken/not taken"—you will not be given a score for Simulations. Simulations cannot be saved before you have finished them, so make sure when you begin that you have 10–15 minutes to dedicate to completing the Simulation.

CONTENTS

For a full listing of the PsykTrek 3.0 Modules available, please visit PsykTrek 3.0 Online.

The Experimental Method

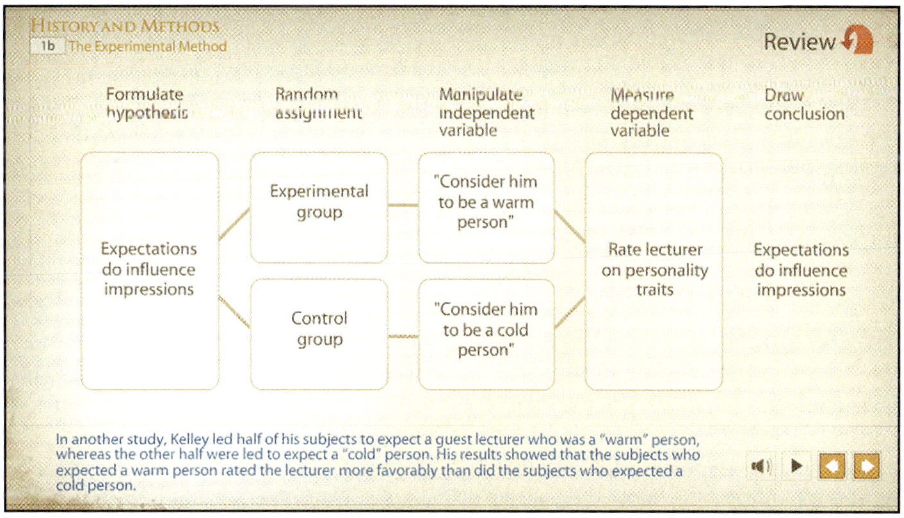

Work through Module 1b (*The Experimental Method*) to enhance your understanding of how research is conducted in psychology.

What's It For?

The experimental method is key in psychological research, and it is quite likely you are already familiar with the way it works. Nevertheless, it's important to be sure you understand dependent and independent variables so that studies you conduct, or ones about which you read, make sense.

Psychology for a Reason: The Experimental Method

An **experiment** is a research method in which the investigator manipulates a **variable** under carefully controlled conditions and observes whether any changes occur in a second variable as a result. *The purpose of an experiment is to find out how one variable (X) affects another variable (Y).* In this formation, X is the independent variable and Y is the dependent variable.

The **independent variable** is the condition or event that an experimenter varies in order to see its impact on another variable. The **dependent variable** is the variable thought to be affected by manipulation of the independent variable. A good shortcut for sorting out the independent and dependent variables is to fit the variables into the equation *"How X affects Y."*

The experimental method generally happens in this order:

1. Formulate a hypothesis.
2. Make a random assignment of experimental group and control group.
3. Manipulate the independent variable by giving the experimental group special treatment while the control group receives no special treatment.
4. Measure the dependent variable by assessing the subjects' behavior (from both groups).
5. Draw a conclusion by answering the question "Does X affect Y?"

It is crucial in any experiment that the experimental and control groups be very similar and that the only difference between them is the treatment they receive in regard to the independent variable. It is only in this way that the experimenter can be assured that the *difference between the groups is based on the manipulation of the independent variable.*

There are, however, many possible variations in experiments. Sometimes, only one group of subjects is used, and they serve as their own control group. The example used in the module shows how to study the effects of distracting music on typing performance. To manipulate the independent variable, you could use the same group and expose them to two different conditions (the presence of distracting music and the lack of distracting music while the same people are typing). In this example, there is only one independent variable: the presence or absence of distracting music.

It is also possible to manipulate two or three independent variables (X_1 X_2 X_3) in a single experiment to examine their joint effects on the dependent variable (Y). To build upon the distracting music example, you could vary both the room temperature and the presence of distracting music. That way you could examine the effects of two variables in one study to see whether the variables interact.

Of course, *you can also use more than one dependent variable (Y_1 Y_2 Y_3) with a single independent variable (X) in a single study.* This approach is frequently used to get a more complete picture of how experimental manipulations affect subjects' behavior.

Practical Solutions

The experimental method has few uses beyond the lab. Remember, it is crucial that the experimental and control groups are very similar. In order for your experiment's results to be reliable (and replicable), you must be certain that only the independent variable is manipulated. That's practically impossible in the real world. However, you probably use the idea behind the experimental method more often than you realize. Suppose you wake up one morning and your car won't start. You don't know that much about mechanics, but you suspect it could be a dead battery. To find out, you would manipulate that one independent variable—the battery's charge—by having a friend use jumper cables to jump the car. If it starts, it was the battery. If it does not, then it's time to move on to manipulate another independent variable. ■

Statistics: Correlation

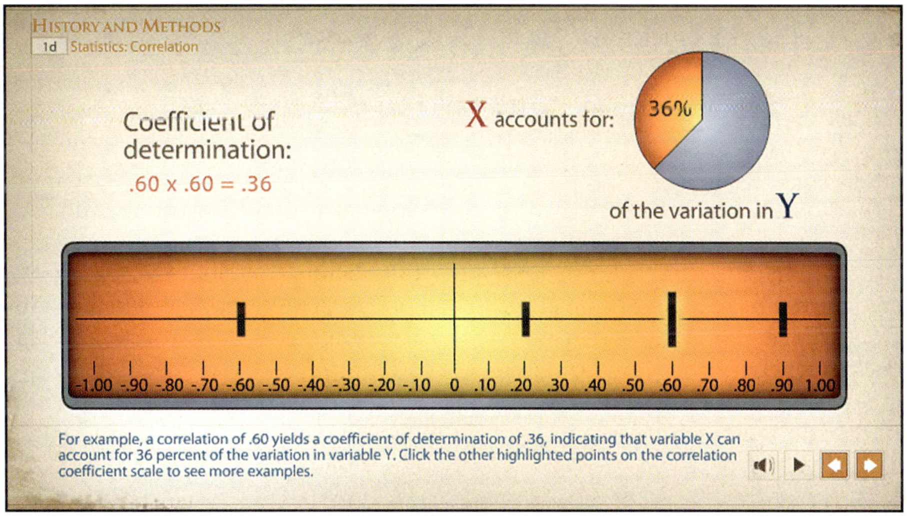

Increase your understanding of correlation by working through Module 1d (*Statistics: Correlation*), which will allow you to plot a scatter diagram and explore numerous examples of correlational relationships.

What's It For?

Remember, the word **correlation** simply refers to a reciprocal relationship between two or more things. The same idea is true when examining statistical correlation in the study of psychology. Understanding the way in which variables correlate is crucial for successful psychological research and interpretation.

Psychology for a Reason: Statistical Correlation

Positive correlations indicate that two variables co-vary in the same direction (a **direct relationship**). This means that high scores on variable X are associated with high scores on variable Y and low scores on variable X are associated with low scores on variable Y. For example, there is a positive correlation between high school grade point average (GPA) and subsequent college GPA.

Negative correlations indicate an inverse relationship between two variables (a **negative-inverse relationship**). This means that people who score high on variable X tend to score low on variable Y, whereas those who score low on X tend to score high on Y. For example, in most college courses there is a negative correlation between how frequently students are absent and how well they perform on exams.

Correlation coefficient is a numerical index of the degree of relationship between two variables. The size of the correlation coefficient varies between zero and plus or minus one. Its size indicates the strength of the association between two variables. The closer the correlation comes to either –1.00 or +1.00, the stronger the relationship.

The direction and strength of correlations can be illustrated graphically in **scatter diagrams**, graphs in which paired X and Y scores for each subject are plotted as single points. When a correlation is perfect, the data points plotted in a scatter diagram fall exactly in a straight line. When the magnitude of a correlation decreases, the data points scatter farther and farther from the straight line that would represent a perfect relationship.

A close link exists between the strength of a correlation and the power it gives scientists to make **predictions**. As a correlation increases in strength, the ability to predict one variable based on knowledge of the other variable increases. That relationship can be quantified precisely. The square of the correlation coefficient is called the **coefficient of determination**. [(Correlation Coefficient)^2 = Coefficient of Determination.] The coefficient of determination indicates percentage of variation in one variable that can be predicted based on the other variable.

Correlation does not equal causation. Although a high correlation facilitates prediction, it does not tell us whether a **cause–effect relationship** exists between the two correlated variables. A correlation between X and Y does not tell us *how* X and Y are related. We do not know whether X causes Y, Y causes X, or both are caused by a third variable, Z. The problem is that *variables can be highly correlated even though they are not causally related*.

Practical Solutions

Sometimes the most absurd examples are great to prove a point. Try this one. As ice cream sales increase, so does the incidence of drowning. Does ice cream somehow cause drowning? Of course not. Both ice cream sales and drowning increase in the summer; the increase in temperature, a larger number of people on vacation, and all sorts of other factors contribute to selling more ice cream and to an increase in drowning. Are there other examples you can think of that might seem to imply causation but are really demonstrating correlation? How about ways in which advertisers might use correlation (and implied causation) to sell products? If you'd like more examples, simply type "causation versus correlation" into your search engine. You'll be amazed by the number of examples people have developed and posted online. ■

The Neuron and the Neural Impulse

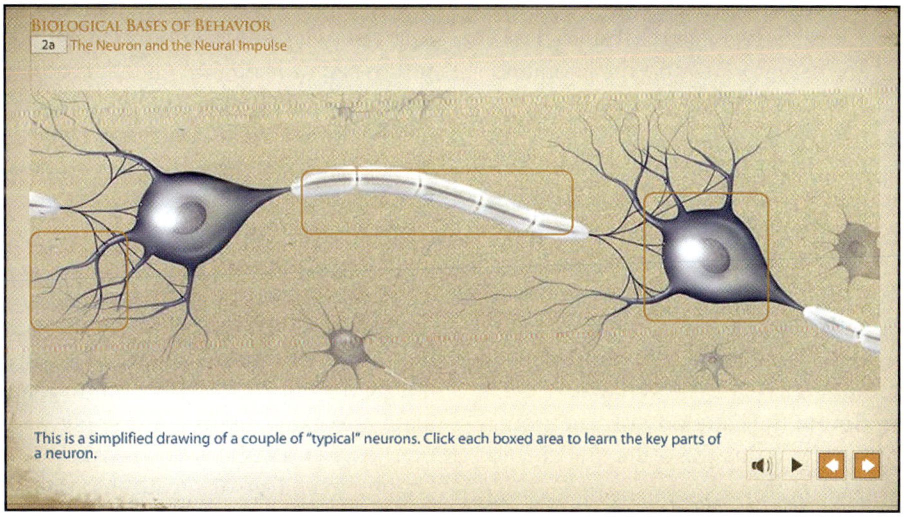

Explore Module 2a (*The Neuron and the Neural Impulse*) to review the various physical components of a neuron.

What's It For?

The **nervous system** is a complex communication network in which signals are constantly being received, integrated, and transmitted; it handles information just as the circulatory system handles blood. It is crucial to understand how information is transmitted through this network in order to understand how interruption in the network affects us. It will help if you can envision the process, imagining the information moving through the network. Module 2a includes outstanding visuals to help you do so.

Psychology for a Reason: Neurons and Neural Impulses

The **nervous system** is divided into the **central nervous system** (the brain and spinal cord) and the **peripheral nervous system**. The peripheral nervous system includes the nerves that lie outside the brain or spinal cord. It is divided into the **somatic nervous system** (which connects to skeletal muscles and to receptors in the skin) and the **autonomic nervous system** (which connects to the heart, blood vessels, smooth muscles, and glands).

The two major types of cells in the nervous system are glia cells and neuron cells. **Glia cells** come in a variety of forms, but their main function is to support the neurons by, among other things, supplying them with nutrients and removing waste material.

Neuron cells receive, integrate, and transmit information. In humans, the vast majority are **interneurons**, or neurons that communicate with other neurons, but others include **sensory neurons**, which receive signals from outside the nervous system, and **motor neurons**, which carry messages from the nervous system to the muscles that move the body. Neuron cells are composed of

- **Dendrites:** parts of a neuron that are specialized to receive information; each individual branch of the structure is a dendrite and the whole branched structure is a **dendritic tree**. (It may help you remember this to know that *dendrite* is derived from the Greek word for "tree branch.") Information flows into the neuron through the dendrites and then away from the neuron along the axon.

- **Axons:** parts of a neuron that are specialized and transmit information to other neurons or to muscles or glands; they are long fibers. Information flows into the neuron through the dendrites, then away from the neuron along the axon. Most human axons are wrapped in a **myelin sheath**; the myelin (a white, fatty substance) serves as an insulator around the axon and speeds the transmission of signals. The axon ends in a cluster of terminal buttons, and inside each button are sacs or vesicles containing **neurotransmitters**, which are chemicals that serve as messengers and may activate neighboring cells. The junction where information is passed from a neuron to another cell is the **synapse**.
- **Soma:** the cell body of a neuron that contains the cell's nuclei.

So those are the buildings blocks of neurons. But to truly understand the process, it helps to think of what neurons actually do. **Neurons at rest** (when not conducting an impulse) are tiny batteries, stores of potential energy. Inside and outside the axon are fluids containing electrically charged atoms and molecules called **ions**. Positively charged **sodium and potassium ions** and negatively charged **chloride ions** are the principal molecules involved in the nerve impulse. The cell membrane itself is **polarized** (it is negatively charged on the inside and positively charged on the outside). The **charge difference**, or **resting potential**, across the membrane can be measured with a pair of microelectrodes connected to an oscilloscope.

Stimulation of a neuron causes **sodium gates** in the cell membrane to open briefly, allowing positively charged sodium ions to run into the axon and cause an upward spike on the oscilloscope screen. This change in charge also causes **potassium gates** to open, and positively charged potassium ions flow out of the neuron. This outflow reestablishes the negative charge inside the axon and causes a drop in the oscilloscope screen. The brief reversal in the charge difference across the neuron membrane (which is seen as a spike on the oscilloscope screen) is called the **action potential** or **neural impulse**.

The **action potential** travels along an axon as sodium gates close and potassium gates open at one point on the membrane, sodium gates are triggered to open at the next point along the axon membrane. The sequential opening of sodium gates at adjacent points moves the action potential along the axon. The **absolute refractory period** occurs because, after the firing of an action potential, some time is needed before the sodium gates are ready to open again. Until they are ready to reopen, the neuron cannot fire. The absolute refractory period is the minimum length of time after an action potential during which another action potential cannot begin; generally this is only about 1 or 2 milliseconds.

Practical Solutions

Multiple sclerosis (MS), which is thought to affect more than 2.5 million people, results from degeneration in some myelin sheaths on axons, which slows or prevents nerve transmission to certain muscles. Go to the National MS Society website at http://www.nationalmssociety.org/index.aspx and explore the site, especially "What Is Multiple Sclerosis?" in the "About MS" section, which has an outstanding video explaining the importance of myelin. Understanding MS, or at least as much as researchers have discovered, will likely be very helpful in increasing your functional knowledge of how neurons work.

MODULE **2c**

Looking Inside the Brain: Research Methods

Go to Module 2c (*Looking Inside the Brain: Research Methods*) to learn how electrical stimulation, lesioning, EEGs, CT scans, PET scans, and MRI scans are used to investigate brain function.

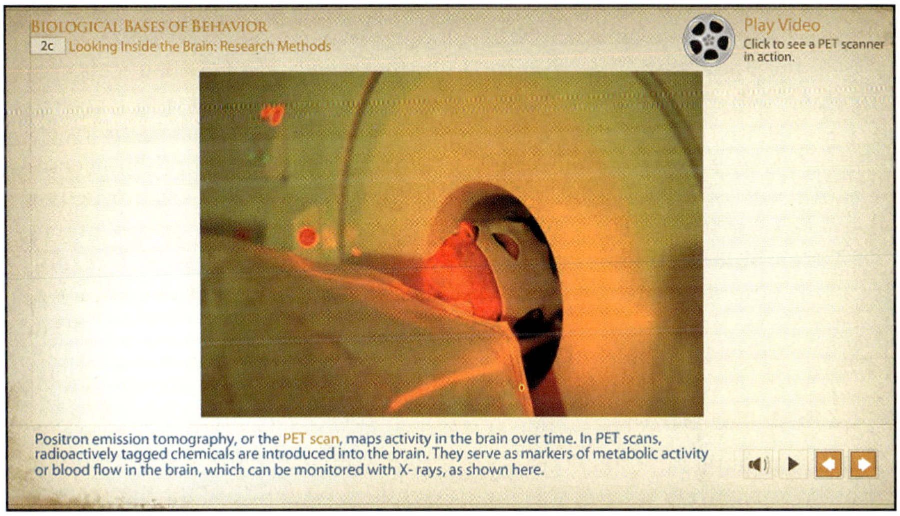

What's It For?

The field of brain research is full of acronyms and quite a bit of Latin. It is worthwhile to make sure you understand the difference between a CT scan and an MRI in order to determine which would be most useful for specific research. Similarly, a grasp of the differences between beta, alpha, theta, and delta waves will enable you to understand just what an EEG can reveal about electrical brain activity.

Psychology for a Reason: Brain Research Methods

EEG is the acronym for **electroencephalograph**, a device that monitors the electrical activity of the brain over time by means of recording electrodes attached to the surface of the scalp. **Brain waves** is the common name for the line tracings that record the EEG results. They vary in **amplitude**, which is indexed by their height, and **frequency**, which is measured in cycles per second (cps). Brain waves are usually divided into four principal bands:

- **Beta waves:** 13-to-24-cps brain waves that are associated with normal waking thought and alert problem solving.
- **Alpha waves:** 8-to-12-cps brain waves that are seen during deep relaxation, when the mind is blank, and during meditation.
- **Theta waves:** 4-to-7-cps brain waves that appear during light sleep.
- **Delta waves:** high-amplitude brain waves (remember, amplitude measures the height of brain waves) under 4 cps that are seen during deep, dreamless sleep.

Scientists sometimes study brain function to observe what happens when specific brain structures in animals are **lesioned**, or disabled. Lesioning is typically done by inserting an electrode into a brain structure and passing a high-frequency electric current through it to burn the tissue and disable the structure. **Stereotaxis instruments** are used by researchers to surgically implant electrodes in exact locations deep inside animals' brains.

ESB is electrical stimulation of the brain that involves sending a weak electric current into a brain structure to activate it. If areas deep within the brain are to be stimulated, the electrodes are implanted using the same stereotaxic techniques used in lesioning procedures. Electrical stimulation studies with animals have made major contributions to the understanding of brain function, such as identifying areas in the brain that contribute to emotional responses as well as so-called pleasure centers, or self-stimulation sites.

CT (computerized tomography) scan is a computer-enhanced X-ray of brain structure. An X-ray beam and an X-ray detector rotate around the patient's head, taking X-rays of the patient's brain from many angles. The computer combines the readings to create vivid images of horizontal slices of the brain.

PET (positron emission tomography) scan maps activity in the brain over time. In PET scans, radioactively tagged chemicals are introduced into the brain. They serve as markers of metabolic activity or blood flow in the brain that can be monitored with X-rays. A PET scan can provide a color-coded map indicating which areas of the brain become active when subjects clench their fists, sing, or do a math problem. PET scans monitor chemical processes and can be used to study the activity of specific neurotransmitters. For example, they have helped researchers map the locations of dopamine pathways in the human brain.

MRI (magnetic resonance imaging) scans use magnetic fields, radio waves, and computerized enhancement to map out brain structure and brain function. MRI scans provide much better images of brain structure than CT scans, producing pictures of the brain that have remarkably high resolution.

Practical Solutions

Chances are you know someone who's had an MRI or a CT scan or maybe even a PET scan. You may have even heard stories about claustrophobes who require the use of "open" MRI machines. But if your physician told you that you needed one of these tests, would you understand the difference? It's worthwhile to understand the way each works in order to understand what each is testing. One way to differentiate at a basic level is to remember that a PET scan focuses on metabolic changes at a cellular level; CT scans and MRIs focus on structural changes. Therefore, PET scans can generally detect abnormalities earlier in their progression. For more on the differences, as well as a good primer on the use of PET scans, visit the Cleveland Clinic website at http://my.clevelandclinic.org/services/PET_Scan/hic_PET_Scan.aspx. ■

Gestalt Psychology

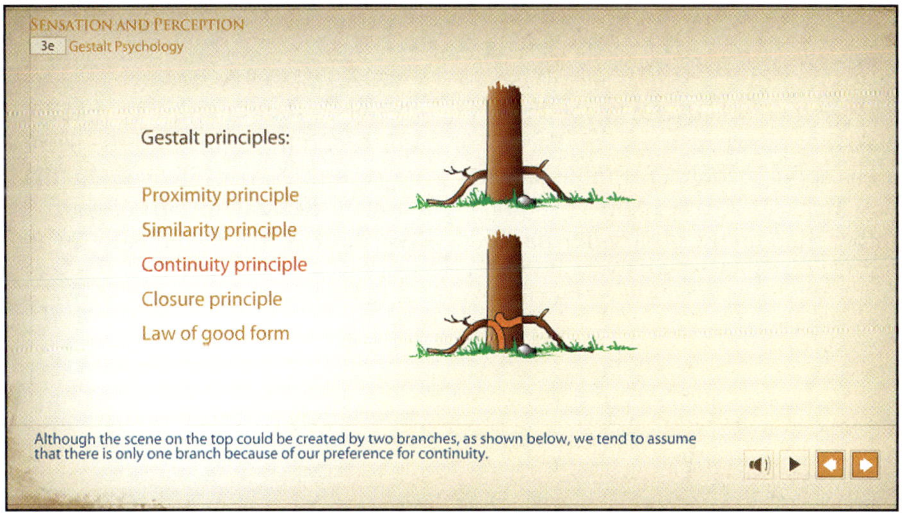

View multiple examples of various Gestalt principles of perception, such as the law of similarity, in Module 3e (*Gestalt Psychology*).

What's It For?

Gestalt psychology is no longer an active theoretical orientation in modern psychology but its influence continues to resonate, and it left a legacy of many useful insights about form perception. You should always remember that Gestalt psychology is different from Gestalt therapy, though obviously the two share many ideas.

Psychology for a Reason: Gestalt Psychology

Gestalt psychology was an influential school of thought that emerged out of Germany, under the leadership of **Max Wertheimer**, during the first half of the 20th century. Gestalt psychologists were very interested in form perception. *Gestalt* is a German word for "form" or "shape." In studying form perception, the Gestaltists repeatedly demonstrated that *the whole can be greater than the sum of its parts.*

Phi phenomenon is an example of the Gestalt principle in which the illusion of movement is created by presenting visual stimuli in rapid succession. It is animation, basically. The animation has a property (motion) that isn't evident in any of its parts (the individual frames).

Figure and ground are two other keys to Gestalt theory. Dividing visual displays into figure and ground is a fundamental way we organize visual perceptions. The figure is the thing being looked at, and the ground is the background against which it stands. Figure and ground are not usually interchangeable, but in a **reversible figure**, they are. The most famous of these is a black-and-white image which is either a white, carved vase on a black background or two black profiles, facing each other, on a white background. What you perceive is determined by what you see as figure and what you see as ground.

Frequently, your visual field may contain many figures sharing a background. Many of the Gestalt principles relate to how these figures are grouped together. Five of these Gestalt principles are:

- **Proximity principle:** people see things that are near to one another as belonging together.

- **Similarity principle:** people tend to group stimuli that are alike.
- **Continuity principle:** people have a tendency to follow in whatever direction they've been led.
- **Closure principle:** people often group elements to create a sense of closure; thus, you may "complete" figures that actually have gaps in them. A circular collection of dashed, curved lines will be perceived as a circle.
- **Law of good form:** people tend to organize forms in the simplest way possible though there are other alternatives; the most general Gestalt principle.

Practical Solutions

Gestalt theory is useful beyond the classroom because of its very basic ideas about visual perception. When you focus your camera on a friend rather than on the library in front of which he's standing, you've made your friend the figure and the library the ground. Notice how you do this many times a day, as part of your everyday life. Were you really aware of this before? For even more fun, go online and search for some Gestalt images.

Visual Illusions

Go to Module 3g (*Visual Illusions*) to play with stunning illusions that will have you questioning your eyes.

What's It For?

Optical illusions clearly demonstrate that human perceptions are not simple reflections of objective reality. Thus, it is apparent that perception is highly subjective. Questions about how we perceive the world around us are central to the study of psychology.

Psychology for a Reason: Visual Illusions

An **optical illusion** involves an apparently inexplicable discrepancy between the appearance of a visual stimulus and its physical reality. Some famous optical illusions include the **Müller-Lyer illusion** in which two vertical lines of identical lengths appear to be very different, which may be caused largely by a perception of depth.

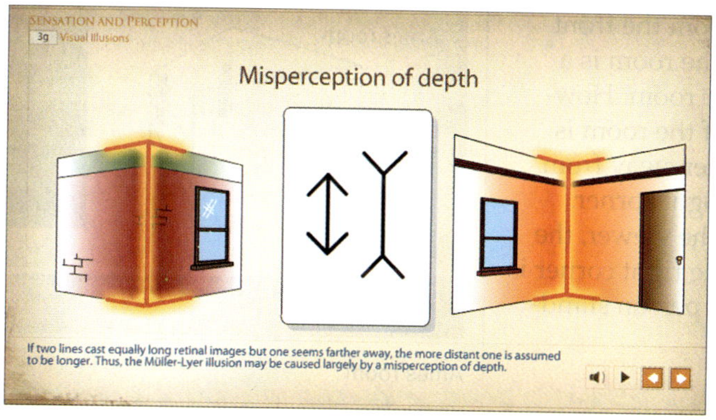

Müller-Lyer illusion

6c MODULE

Physiology of Memory

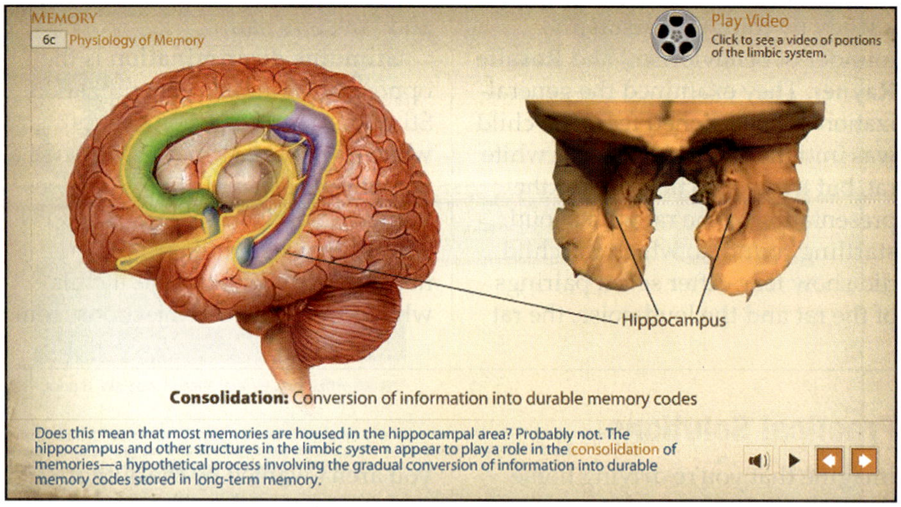

Examine what we know about the neurological bases of memory by accessing Module 6c (*Physiology of Memory*).

What's It For?

To make sense of this topic, be sure you have reviewed synaptic transmission; visit Module 2b (*Synaptic Transmission*) to refresh your memory before viewing Module 6c. Understanding this module can help you determine the best way to study before exams.

Psychology for a Reason: Physiology of Memory

The physiology of memory is not an exact science. Past research has not always led to significant discoveries, and current research takes many paths. Two of those research paths are biochemistry of memory and neural circuitry of memory.

- **Biochemistry of memory** is a line of research that suggests that specific memories depend on biochemical changes that occur at specific **synapses**. **Eric Kandel** and his colleagues have studied conditioned reflexes in a simple sea slug that has large neurons that are relatively easy to work with. These studies have shown that specific forms of learning in the sea slug result in an increase or decrease in the release of neurotransmitters by **presynaptic neurons**. Kandel believes that durable changes in synaptic transmission may be the building blocks of more complex memories as well.
- **Neural circuitry of memory** research by **Richard Thompson** and his colleagues have found promising leads. They have shown that specific memories may depend on localized neural circuits in the brain by studying the **eyeblink response** in rabbits. The key link in this circuit is a microscopic spot in the **cerebellum**. When this spot is destroyed, the conditioned stimulus no longer elicits the eyeblink response, even though the unconditioned stimulus still does. This finding does not mean that the cerebellum is the key to all memory. Thompson theorizes that other memories

probably create entirely different pathways in other areas of the brain.

Organic amnesia is extensive memory loss due to a head injury. There are two types, retrograde and anterograde. The study of both has greatly increased our knowledge of how memory works.

In **retrograde amnesia**, a person loses memories for events that occurred prior to the injury. In **anterograde amnesia**, a person loses memories for events that occur after the injury. (An easy way to remember the difference is that *retro* means "past, backward"—so in retrograde amnesia, a person loses memories from before his or her injury.)

Cases of anterograde amnesia have been outstanding sources of information about the brain and memory and have provided evidence that damage to the **hippocampus** and nearby structures in the brain contributes to anterograde amnesia. Interestingly, hippocampal damage has a severe impact on the **declarative memory system**, which handles factual information such as names, dates, faces, events, and ideas. The **procedural memory system**, which handles memory for actions and skills such as bike riding and typing, may be largely unaffected. This does not mean that memories are housed in the hippocampal region. Instead, it appears that the hippocampus and other structures in the **limbic system** play a role in the consolidation of memories, a hypothetical process involving the gradual conversion of information into durable memory codes stored in long-term memory. So where are memories stored? Theorists suspect that memories are stored in the same cortical areas that were originally involved in processing the sensory input that led to the memories. So, for instance, memories of visual information may be stored in areas of the visual cortex.

Practical Solutions

So how do *you* learn and store memories most effectively? Think about the years you have spent in a classroom. Do you find you are more successful in remembering classroom information from hearing it or seeing it? Or is it some combination of the two? If listening is most useful, then you are likely an auditory learner, and traditional lectures work well for you. If seeing is more helpful, then you are likely a visual learner, and you may find that films, diagrams, and charts are more useful. Or you may find that certain types of input work better for certain types of information. Whether your classroom days end with college, or you spend your career in one as a teacher, understanding the physiology of memory, or at least the current theories, will improve your grasp of your own and others' learning styles. And who wouldn't like to make better grades?

7B MODULE

Key Concepts in Testing With Simulation 8, Psychological Testing: Measuring Your Creativity

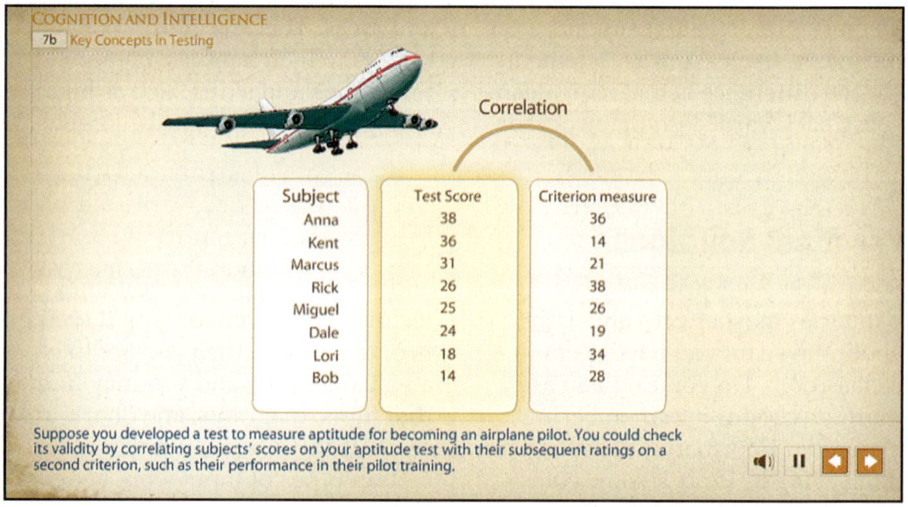

Review how psychometricians assess the reliability and validity of psychological tests in Module 7b (*Key Concepts in Testing*).

What's It For?

Can a reliable test be invalid? Can an invalid test be highly reliable? What role do variables play in designing a psychological test? What is a "standardized test"? What is a percentile score? By understanding the answers to these questions, you may just perform better on these types of tests (or at least have a better grasp of what your test results really tell you), or you may even find you have a knack for designing psychological tests.

Psychology for a Reason: Key Concepts in Testing

Personality scales and **tests of mental abilities** are both standardized measures of behavior. **Standardization** refers to the uniform procedures used in the administration and scoring of a test. For example, people taking the same test from different examiners in different locations get the same instructions, the same questions, the same time limits, and so on, so their scores can be meaningfully compared.

Test norms provide information on where a score on a psychological test ranks in relation to other scores on that test. Usually, test norms allow you to convert your raw score on a test into a percentile. Your **percentile score** indicates the percentage of people who score at or below the score you have obtained.

Reliability refers to the measurement consistency of a test or other kinds of measurement techniques. It may make it easier to remember this concept if you note that any kind of measuring device (a tire gauge, a stopwatch, or a psychological test) should be reasonably consistent.

Test–retest reliability is the most widely used approach to check a test's reliability. It is estimated by comparing subjects' scores on two administrations of a test. For example, to check the test–retest reliability of a newly developed test of assertiveness, we could ask a group of subjects to take the test on two occasions a few weeks apart. If the subjects have similar scores on the first and second tests, the test's reliability is high. If the subjects have very different scores on the first and second tests, the test is inconsistent and has low reliability.

Correlation coefficient is a numerical index of the degree of relationship between two variables. A precise reliability estimate requires the computation of a correlation coefficient. In estimates of test–retest reliability, the two variables that must be correlated are the two sets of scores from the two administrations of the test. If people have relatively similar scores on the two administrations, this consistency yields a substantial positive correlation. The closer the correlation comes to +1.00, the more reliable the test.

Validity refers to the ability of a test to measure what it was designed to measure, which is different from reliability. In other words, even if a test is highly reliable, is it valid? There are three types of validity that we might check:

- **Content validity** is the degree to which the content of a test is representative of the domain it is supposed to cover. Imagine a poorly prepared physics exam that includes questions on material that was not covered in class or in assigned reading. The professor has compromised the validity of the exam, even though it might be a reliable exam.
- **Criterion-related validity** is estimated by correlating subjects' scores on a test with their scores on an independent criterion of the trait assessed by the test. Psychological tests are often used to predict individuals' performance in college, training programs, jobs, and so on. For example, if you developed a test to measure aptitude for becoming an airplane pilot, you could check its validity by correlating subjects' scores on your aptitude test with their subsequent ratings on a second criterion, such as their performance in their pilot training. If your test has high validity, people who score high on the test should earn high performance ratings and low scorers should achieve low ratings. But if little or no relationship exists between the two sets of scores, criterion-related validity is low and the test apparently does not measure what it was designed to measure.
- **Construct validity** is the extent to which there is evidence that a test measures a particular hypothetical construct. Many psychological tests attempt to measure abstract qualities such as creativity.

Practical Solutions

If you're in college, you've probably taken the SAT. But what, exactly, does the SAT measure? What's your best guess? Is it intelligence? Is it aptitude? If so, aptitude for what? The SAT is actually a quite controversial test. Perform an online search with the phrase "What does the SAT measure?" and see what kinds of results you find. Be sure to check out the PBS series *Frontline* site, as well as the collegeboard.com site. Does the SAT measure what you thought it did?

Then, go to Simulation 8 (*Psychological Testing: Measuring Your Creativity*) where you can take the Remote Associates Test (RAT), developed in 1959 by Sarnoff and Martha Mednick to measure creativity. You can then compare your score with others and find out more about validity in testing. ■

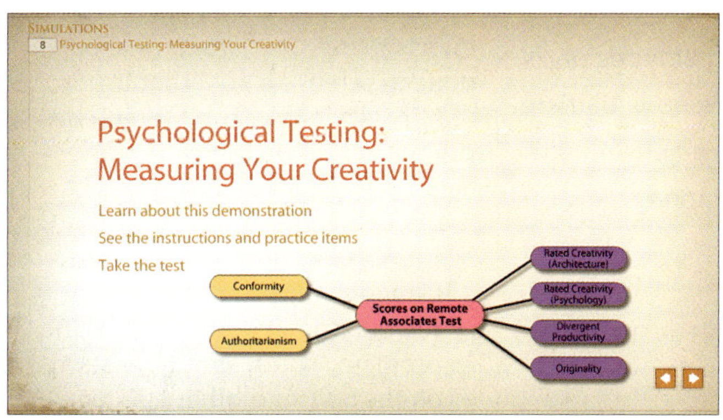

Simulation 8: Psychological Testing: Measuring Your Creativity

7E MODULE

Problem Solving With Simulation 7: Problem Solving

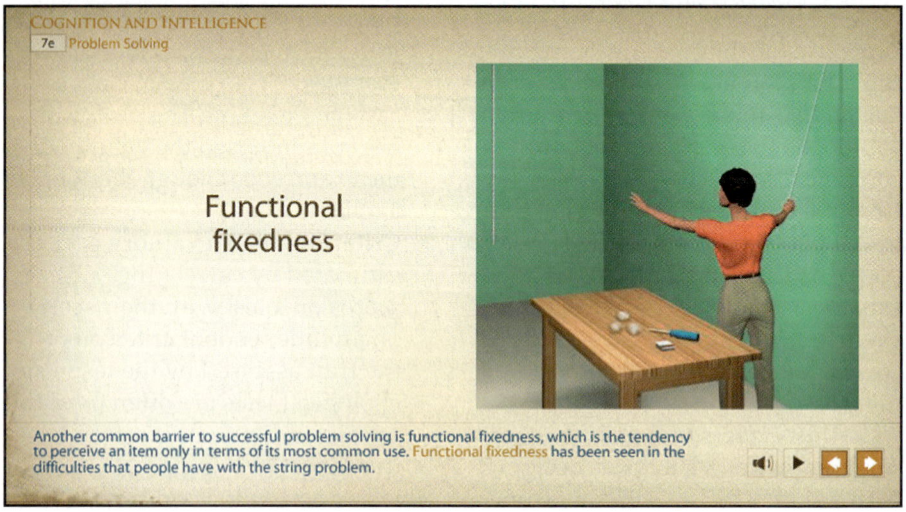

Work through Module 7e (*Problem Solving*) to see how various barriers to effective problem solving often thwart our efforts.

What's It For?

We all solve problems every day and an understanding of types of problems, as well as various barriers to problem solving, is an asset both in and out of the classroom.

Psychology for a Reason: Problem Solving

Problem solving refers to active efforts to discover what must be done to achieve a goal that is not readily attainable. **Jim Greeno** has proposed that problems can be categorized into three basic classes.

- In **problems of inducing structure**, you must discover the relations among the parts of the problem. Think about questions on the SAT and other standardized tests where you are asked to complete a series of letters or numbers. You must determine the pattern in the existing series in order to determine the next in the series. In other words, you must induce (infer by deductive reasoning) a structure.
- In **problems of arrangement**, you must arrange the parts in a way that satisfies some criterion. The parts can be arranged in many ways but only one or a few of the arrangements form a solution. Studies have shown that arrangement problems are often solved with a **burst of insight** rather than through careful planning.
- In **problems of transformation**, you must carry out a sequence of transformations in order to reach a specific goal. Like arrangement problems, transformation problems consist of an initial state and a goal. The difference is that in transformation problems the problem solver knows exactly what the goal is. Problems of transformation tend to be solved by carrying out a **planned sequence** of steps rather than by sudden insight.

But psychologists have identified a number of **barriers** that frequently impede subjects' efforts to arrive at solutions to problems. Some types of barriers follow:

- **Irrelevant information** is information that leads many people astray. For example, people often incorrectly assume that all numerical information in a problem is necessary to solve it. Effective problem solving requires that you attempt to figure out what information is relevant and what is irrelevant before proceeding.
- **Functional fixedness** is the tendency to perceive an item only in terms of its most common use. In one of the sample problems on PsykTrek, you have a selection of items to use to solve a problem; these items include a book of matches, some cotton balls, and a screwdriver. To solve the problem, you must use one of those items in a way that you would not normally use it. You must overcome your functional fixedness, your perception that an item has limited functions. Remember the television show *MacGyver,* where the lead character could seemingly solve any life-threatening situation with nothing more than a pair of nail clippers, a gym sock, and a soda can (or some other odd assortment of items)? MacGyver consistently overcame functional fixedness.
- **Rigid thinking** is at work when a mental set interferes with effective problem solving. A **mental set** exists when people persist in using problem-solving strategies that have worked in the past. An example is when you are confronted with a series of the same type of problem. If a certain strategy works for solving the first few of these problems, you are likely to continue using that strategy for the next in the series, even if there is a simpler solution that is rather obvious. You become reliant on the "tried and true" strategy used in the first few problems.
- People often make assumptions that impose **unnecessary restraints** on problem-solving efforts. This happens when, even though a problem's parameters are clearly defined, you may not readily see options that are *not excluded by the parameters*.

Practical Solutions

It is easy to see the value of problem solving beyond psychology. You solve problems every day. Many standardized tests measure problem-solving ability. To see a classic problem that psychologists have studied extensively, try your hand at Simulation 7, which presents the Hobbits and Orcs problem, a modern twist on the classic.

Theories of Emotion

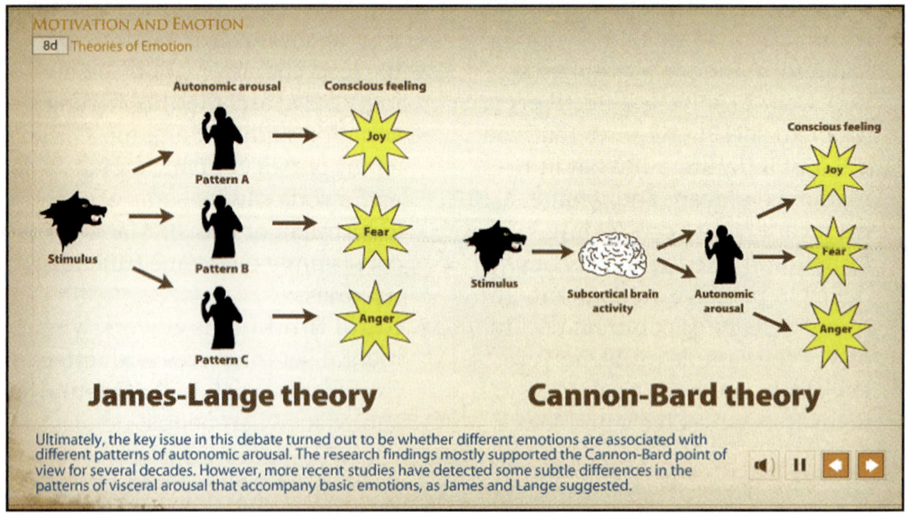

Check out Module 8d (*Theories of Emotion*) to enhance your understanding of the James-Lange, Cannon-Bard, and two-factor theories of emotion.

What's It For?

Understanding emotions, including how they are triggered, how our minds and bodies process them, and the role that evolution plays in emotional responses, still eludes researchers. But the information presented here is a good primer on what major theorists have to offer. Which do you find more convincing?

Psychology for a Reason: Theories of Emotion

First, here are a couple of basic definitions. **Autonomic** means "acting or occurring involuntarily." **Visceral** means "not intellectual; instinctive" (and is derived from the Latin *viscera*, meaning "the internal organs").

In the 1880s William James and Carl Lange both concluded independently that the conscious experience of emotion results from one's perception of **autonomic arousal**. Common sense suggests that if you stumble onto a growling wild dog in the woods, you experience the emotion of fear, which leads to autonomic arousal. The **James-Lange theory of emotion** turned this idea upside down by asserting that the perception of autonomic arousal leads to the experience of fear. The "commonsense" view assumes your pulse is racing because you're fearful; the James-Lange theory argued that you're fearful because your pulse is racing. Therefore, the James-Lange theory states that different patterns of autonomic activation lead to the experience of different emotions.

Walter Cannon disagreed with the James-Lange theory and argued that autonomic changes are too slow to precede the conscious experience of emotion. So, in 1927 he proposed a different explanation, which Philip Bard built upon in 1934. The **Cannon-Bard theory** argues that emotion occurs when subcortical brain structures send signals simultaneously to the cortex, creating the conscious experience of emotion, and to the autonomic nervous system, creating **visceral arousal**. The theory posits that people experiencing very different emotions, such as joy, fear, and anger, exhibit almost identical patterns of autonomic arousal.

The key issue in this debate is whether different emotions are associated with different patterns of autonomic arousal. The research findings mostly supported the Cannon-Bard theory for several decades but more recent studies have detected some subtle differences in the patterns of visceral arousal that accompany basic emotions, as James and Lange suggested.

In the 1960s, Stanley Schachter argued that people look at situational cues to differentiate between alternative emotions. According to his **two-factor theory**, the experience of emotions depends on two factors: autonomic arousal and one's cognitive appraisal of that arousal. He proposes that when you experience visceral arousal, you search your environment for an explanation.

Some theorists have returned to Darwinian ideas to explain emotional responses. Darwin believed that emotions developed because of their adaptive value (fear would help an organism avoid danger, aiding in its survival). This Darwinian view, that human emotions are a product of evolution, is the foundation for several **evolutionary theories** of emotion developed independently by S. S. Tomkins, Carroll Izard, and Robert Plutchik. Like the **Cannon-Bard theory**, these evolutionary theories consider emotions to be largely innate reactions that originate in subcortical brain structures. As such, emotions should be recognizable under most conditions without much thought. After all, primitive animals that are incapable of complex thought seem to have little difficulty recognizing their emotions.

Evolutionary theorists assume that evolution has equipped humans with a small number of innate emotions with proven adaptive value. Their principal question is: What are the fundamental emotions?

- Tomkins would answer: fear, anger, enjoyment, disgust, interest, surprise, contempt, shame, and distress.
- Izard would answer: fear, anger, joy, disgust, interest, surprise, contempt, shame, sadness, and guilt.
- Plutchik would answer: fear, anger, joy, disgust, anticipation, surprise, sadness, and acceptance.

All three theorists agree that there are between 8 and 10 **primary emotions**, and 6 of those are on each theorist's list (fear, anger, joy, disgust, interest, and surprise). But of course people experience more than 8 or 10 emotions. Evolutionary theorists account for other emotions by suggesting there are **blends of emotions**—for example, fear and surprise blend into secondary emotions, such as awe. Think of it as you would a color chart: All colors can be derived from different mixtures of primary colors. Plutchik also suggests that emotions might involve one primary emotion with experiences at different levels of intensity. For example, apprehension, fear, and terror are viewed as different intensities of the same primary emotion.

Practical Solutions

Even though understanding emotions may still be beyond our reach, recognizing emotions is a necessary skill. In fact, researchers and designers are working to develop computer systems that can recognize human emotions. To find out more about some of these efforts, check out *Carnegie Mellon's Robotics Institute* and its Facial Expression Analysis page at http://www.ri.cmu.edu/research_project. Then read through the abstract on "Human and computer recognition of facial expressions of emotion" at *ScienceDirect* at http://www.sciencedirect.com.

Based upon what you've learned about the complexities of understanding how emotions work, what challenges do you think these researches have and will face? What types of applications would benefit from this type of computer system?

Kohlberg's Theory of Moral Development

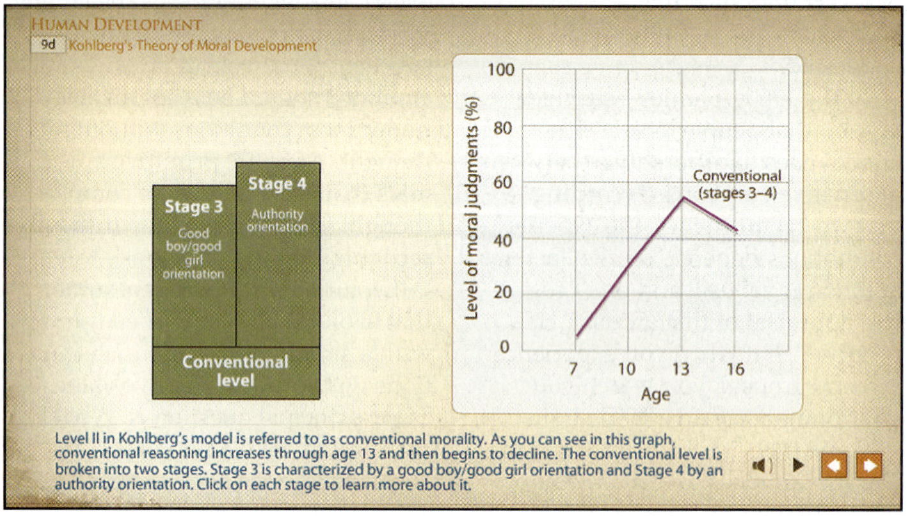

Enhance your appreciation of Lawrence Kohlberg's analyses of moral reasoning by exploring Module 9d (*Kohlberg's Theory of Moral Development*).

What's It For?

Like so many aspects of psychology, Kohlberg's theory of moral development is just that—a theory. Other researchers have questioned his conclusions, but the influence of his theory remains. As you read through the main points, think about what you would consider to be "questionable" aspects of the theory.

Psychology for a Reason: Kohlberg's Theory of Moral Development

Lawrence Kohlberg is the architect of an influential model that describes developmental changes in youngsters' reasoning about right and wrong. He built upon Jean Piaget's earlier work, which argued that the way youngsters think about moral issues is determined by their level of cognitive development.

Kohlberg's theory focuses on **moral reasoning** rather than overt behavior. He presented his subjects with thorny moral questions, such as **Heinz's dilemma** (which you can read in full on PsykTrek). After presenting subjects with a complex moral dilemma, Kohlberg would ask them what the actor in the dilemma should do and, more important, why. The "why" is what truly interested Kohlberg.

Based upon his research, Kohlberg concluded that people progress through a series of **three levels of moral development**, each of which can be broken into two sublevels, yielding a total of six stages. Each stage represents a different approach to thinking about right and wrong.

- **Preconventional morality—Level 1:** Preconventional reasoning declines as children grow older. The preconventional level is broken into two stages. *Stage 1* is characterized by a punishment orientation, and *Stage 2*, by a naïve reward orientation. Children in Stage 1 pay little attention to people's intentions in judging morality. The need to avoid punishment is the main reason for moral behavior. Right and wrong are determined by what is punished. Children in Stage 2 are motivated to share with others or comply with rules in order to gain tangible returns. Right and wrong are determined by what is rewarded.

- **Conventional morality—Level II:** Conventional reasoning increases through age 13 and then begins to decline. As with all levels, this one has two stages. *Stage 3* is characterized by a good boy/good girl orientation, and *Stage 4*, by an authority orientation. Youngsters in Stage 3 comply with rules to promote harmony in their personal relationships. The main reason for behaving morally is to win the approval of friends and relatives for being a "virtuous person." Right and wrong are determined by others' approval or disapproval. Youngsters in Stage 4 comply with rules to promote order in their society. They are motivated to behave morally because they understand that rules are necessary for maintaining social order. Right and wrong are determined by society's rules and laws. These rules are viewed as inflexible guidelines that should be obeyed rigidly.
- **Postconventional morality—Level III:** Postconventional reasoning begins around age 10 and increases during adolescence. The postconventional level is composed of *Stage 5*, characterized by a social contract orientation, and *Stage 6*, characterized by individual principles and conscience orientation. In Stage 5, people are motivated to behave morally because they understand that laws are necessary for social order, but laws are viewed as fallible expressions of the will of the majority rather than absolute rules that must be followed rigidly. In thinking about right and wrong, there is the beginning of a distinction between what is legal and what is moral. In Stage 6 people conform to internal principles to avoid self-condemnation. They define right and wrong in terms of abstract ethical principles that emphasize equity, justice, and the dignity of human beings. They clearly distinguish between what is legal and what is moral.

Practical Solutions

Whether or not you agree with Kohlberg's theory (and plenty of online sources offer criticisms of it), you should become comfortable with questioning any theory you encounter. Remember, academic research and conclusions such as Kohlberg's are part of an evolving academic discourse on a topic, no matter the academic discipline. Some of the questions you might ask about Kohlberg's theory include: What is his definition of morality? Can there be different definitions of morality? Is morality subjective depending upon one's culture? Is morality subjective depending upon the time in which a person lived? What role does the concept of justice play in Kohlberg's theory? Does justice have a universally agreed-upon definition?

10D MODULE

Biological Theory

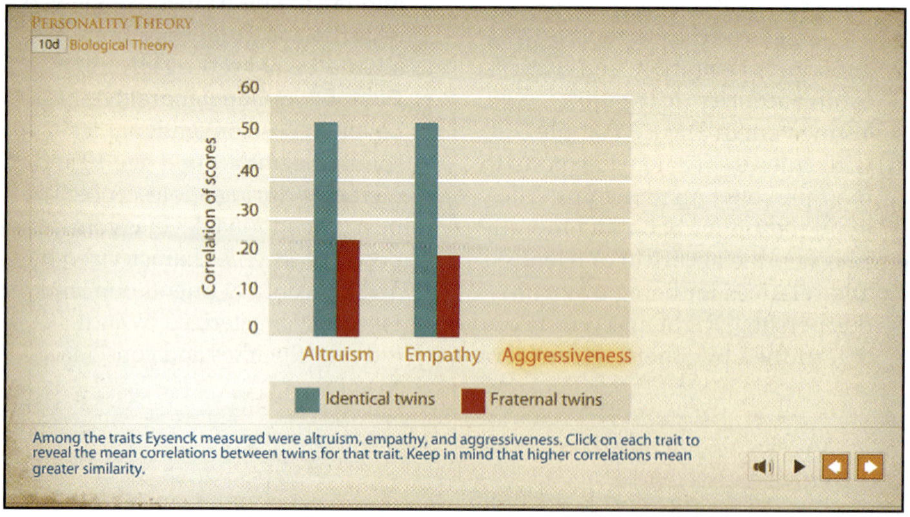

Learn more about Hans Eysenck's model of personality by working through Module 10d (*Biological Theory*).

What's It For?

If you are a shy, introverted person who prefers books to parties, why do you possess those traits? Is it because you were born that way or because your parents encouraged reading and discouraged social activities? Or perhaps you were horribly embarrassed in your third-grade play and never sought the spotlight again? Psychologists who study biological theories try to find answers to those questions, to answer the question of "nature versus nurture."

Psychology for a Reason: Biological Theory

In the 1940s, **William Sheldon** attempted to link physique to personality on the grounds that both are governed by genetic endowment. To do so, he identified three body types. **Endomorphy** referred to the degree to which a person's body was fat, round, and soft. **Mesomorphy** referred to a hard, strong, muscular body type. **Ectomorphy** referred to a thin, flat, frail body type. Sheldon's theory was based on research in which he found high correlations between body type and certain clusters of personality traits.

- **Endomorphic:** sociable, relaxed, affectionate, and even-tempered
- **Mesomorphic:** energetic, competitive, aggressive, and bold
- **Ectomorphic:** inhibited, apprehensive, intellectual, introverted, and self-conscious

But Sheldon's findings could not be replicated, and it became clear that his research was marred by **experimenter bias**. In making his personality ratings, he was influenced by his subjects' readily apparent physiques, and he saw what he expected to see.

Hans Eysenck views personality structure as a **hierarchy of traits** in which many superficial traits are derived from a smaller number of more basic traits, which are derived from a handful of fundamental higher-order traits, such as extroversion. He maintains that personality is largely determined by a person's genes and links heredity to personality, in part, through conditioning concepts borrowed from the behavioral approach. Some people can acquire conditioned responses more readily than others because of inherited differences in their physiological functioning. These variations influence people's conditioned emotional responses, which shape their personality. For example, Eysenck believes that people who condition easily acquire more conditioned fears and inhibitions than others and thus are more likely to become introverted.

Behavioral genetics research has provided evidence consistent with Eysenck's assertion that personality is molded by **heredity**. In one twin study, 573 pairs of twins responded to a number of personality scales. Among the traits measured were altruism, empathy, and aggressiveness. Consistent with the genetic view, identical twins were found to be much more similar than fraternal twins on all three traits. But skeptics raised questions. Was genetic similarity the true cause for the greater personality resemblance between identical twins? After all, identical twins are treated more alike than fraternal twins. Was it environment or heredity that was responsible for the identical twins' greater personality similarity? A University of Minnesota study was a landmark in attempting to answer this question by comparing twins reared apart versus those reared together.

The **Minnesota study** was the first to administer the same personality test to identical and fraternal twins reared apart and to those reared together. The results concluded that identical twins reared together were more similar than fraternal twins reared together. But more important, *identical twins reared apart were found to be more similar to each other than fraternal twins reared together.* This means it is unlikely that identical twins exhibit greater personality resemblance than fraternal twins because they are treated more alike. The Minnesota test results provide strong support for Eysenck's claim that personality is largely inherited.

Practical Solutions

Most of us have heard of what is called the nature versus nurture debate, the argument over what is more influential in determining our personalities—heredity or environment? You may even have an opinion on this debate. But the Human Genome Project brought a new twist to that debate. For more about how, visit the PBS Nova site, entitled "Nature vs Nurture Revisited," at http://www.pbs.org/wgbh/nova/genome/debate.html. For more information on the 13-year-long project itself, visit the Human Genome Project Information page at http://www.ornl.gov/sci/techresources/Human_Genome/project/about.shtml. Does the preliminary information about the Human Genome Project on the PBS site change your opinion? If you had no opinion before, does the information help you form one?

11A MODULE

Anxiety Disorders

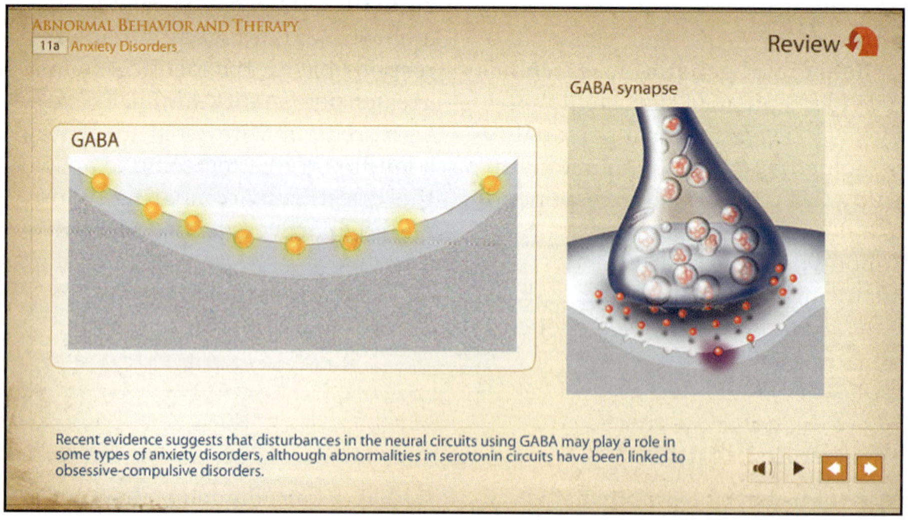

Visit Module 11a (*Anxiety Disorders*) to dig deeper into the nature and causes of anxiety-dominated disturbances and to see a patient describe his panic attacks.

What's It For?

It is quite likely that you know someone who has been diagnosed with an anxiety disorder, and much of the terminology in this module will be familiar. Psychologists have classified these disorders and examined their differences in order to theorize how to best treat those who suffer from them.

Psychology for a Reason: Anxiety Disorders

Anxiety disorders are a class of disorders marked by chronic, troublesome feelings of excessive apprehension and anxiety. Studies show these disorders are quite common, occurring in roughly 19% of the population. There are four principal types of anxiety disorders. (Note that PsykTrek includes the full DSM-IV Diagnostic Criteria for each of these disorder types.)

- **Generalized anxiety disorder** is marked by a chronic, high level of anxiety that is not tied to a specific threat. The anxiety is frequently accompanied by physical symptoms, such as dizziness, sweating, and heart palpitations.
- **Phobic disorder** is marked by a persistent and irrational fear of an object or situation that presents no realistic danger. Although mild phobias are very common, people are said to have a phobic disorder when their fears seriously interfere with everyday functioning. Some phobias are acrophobia (fear of heights) or claustrophobia (fear of small, enclosed spaces).
- **Panic disorder** is characterized by recurrent attacks of overwhelming anxiety that usually occur suddenly and unexpectedly. After a number of attacks, victims' concern about exhibiting panic in public may escalate to the point where they are afraid to leave home. This creates agoraphobia, which is a fear of going out to public places. (In addition to the DSM-IV Criteria for Panic Disorder with Agoraphobia, PsykTrek also includes a case study, and a video in which a person describes a panic attack.)

- **Obsessive-compulsive disorder** is marked by persistent, uncontrollable intrusions of unwanted thoughts called obsessions and urges to engage in senseless rituals called compulsions. Compulsions involve stereotyped rituals, such as constant hand washing or endless rechecking of locks, faucets, and the like.

In studies of anxiety disorders, investigators examine many complicated interactions. In studies that assess the impact of heredity, investigators look at concordance rates. A **concordance rate** indicates the percentage of twin pairs or other pairs of relatives that exhibit the same disorder. If identical twins, who share more genetic similarity, show higher concordance rates than fraternal twins, who share less genetic overlap, this finding supports the genetic hypothesis. Major studies suggest that heredity can create a predisposition to anxiety disorders.

Evidence also suggests that a link may exist between anxiety disorders and **neurotransmitter activity** in the brain. Therapeutic drugs that reduce excessive anxiety, such as Valium, appear to increase inhibitory activity at **GABA (the neurotransmitter gamma-aminobutyric acid) synapses**. This finding suggests that disturbances in the neural circuits using GABA may play a role in some types of anxiety disorders.

Obsessive compulsive symptoms can be reduced by drugs that inhibit the **reuptake of serotonin** and thus increase activity at **serotonin synapses**. This evidence suggests that abnormally low levels of activity in some serotonin circuits may contribute to obsessive-compulsive disorders. You may have heard the term "selective serotonin reuptake inhibitors," or SSRIs; Prozac is probably the best known of these.

Many anxiety responses, especially phobias, may be acquired through **classical conditioning**. If a neutral stimulus, such as an elevator, is paired with a frightening event, such as the elevator dropping a couple of feet, it may become a conditioned stimulus eliciting fear.

After a fear is acquired, people often start avoiding the anxiety-producing stimulus, such as taking the stairs instead of the elevator. This **avoidance response** consistently leads to **negative reinforcement** because it alleviates the person's conditioned fear. Thus, the avoidance response is strengthened, and the person does not have an opportunity to unlearn the conditioned fear.

Cognitive theorists maintain that certain styles of thinking make some people particularly vulnerable to anxiety disorders. According to these theorists, some people are more likely to suffer from problems with anxiety because they tend to misinterpret harmless situations as threatening, focus excessive attention on perceived threats, and selectively recall information that seems threatening.

Recent studies also suggest that high stress can help precipitate the onset of anxiety disorders.

Practical Solutions

If you've never heard of Prozac, you're in a tiny minority. Introduced in 1986, this drug has become practically synonymous with antidepressants of any name. But now that you know a bit more about anxiety disorders, go to the Prozac homepage at http://www.prozac.com/index.jsp and read through the information you find there. What are the FDA-approved uses for Prozac? What do these disorders have in common? Do the side effects seem to outweigh the risks for some of the disorders treated with Prozac?

11D MODULE

Insight Therapies

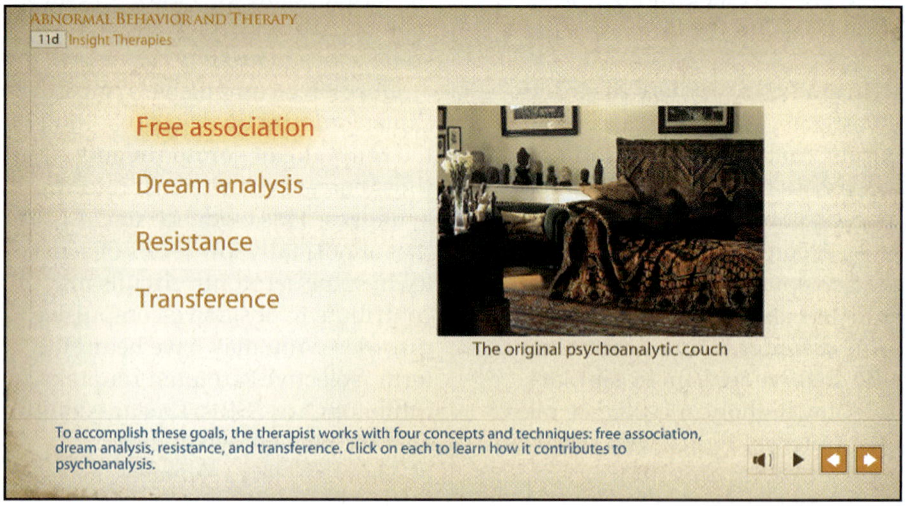

Explore Module 11d (*Insight Therapies*) to enhance your understanding of psychoanalysis.

What's It For?

The professional treatment of psychological disorders and problems is called **psychotherapy**. Although therapeutic procedures are exceedingly diverse approaches to treatment, they can be classified into three broad categories: insight therapies, behavioral therapies, and biomedical therapies. The focus here is on insight therapies, specifically psychoanalysis and client-centered therapy.

Psychology for a Reason: Insight Therapies

There are many systems of **insight therapies**, including psychotherapy and client-centered therapy. All involve **talk therapy**, the goal of which is to pursue increased insight regarding the nature of the client's difficulties and to sort through possible solutions.

Psychoanalysis is the original insight therapy, devised over 100 years ago by **Sigmund Freud**. He mostly treated anxiety-dominated disturbances that were then called **neuroses**. Freud believed that neurotic problems are caused by conflicts left over from early childhood and are buried in the depths of the vast unconscious. He thought that these inner conflicts involved battles among the **id**, **ego**, and **superego**, usually over sexual and aggressive impulses. He theorized that people depend on **defense mechanisms** to avoid confronting these conflicts, but he asserted that defenses tend to be only partially successful, leaving neurotic individuals troubled by anxiety and guilt. The Freudian analyst attempts to probe the depths of the unconscious to discover unresolved conflicts. Psychoanalysis can be a slow and painful process of self-examination, routinely requiring 3 to 5 years. (See the module for a brief summary of an actual case.) To accomplish this, the therapist works with four concepts and techniques.

- **Free association** happens when clients spontaneously express their thoughts and feelings exactly as they occur, regardless of how trivial, silly, or embarrassing they might be. The analyst searches for clues about what is going on in the client's unconscious.

- In **dream analysis**, clients are trained to remember their dreams, which they describe in therapy. The therapist analyzes the symbolism in the dreams to interpret their meaning.
- **Resistance** is composed of the client's largely unconscious defensive maneuvers intended to hinder therapy's progress. Clients exhibit resistance because they don't want to face painful, disturbing conflicts buried in their unconscious.
- **Transference** occurs when clients relate to their therapist in ways that mimic critical relationships in their lives. Psychoanalysts often encourage transference so clients can reenact crucial relationships in the context of therapy with the goal of bringing repressed feelings and conflicts to the surface, allowing the client to work through them.

Many variations on Freud's original approach have developed over the years. These descendants are known collectively as **psychodynamic therapies**. About 25% of psychologists continue to use psychodynamic approaches, while about 6% practice client-centered therapy.

Carl Rogers, a prominent humanistic theorist, developed **client-centered therapy** in the 1940s and 1950s. He maintains that most personal distress is due to **incongruence**, or the disparity between a person's self-concept and reality. Incongruence makes people feel threatened by realistic feedback about themselves, leading to recurrent anxiety. This anxiety often spawns defensive behavior intended to protect one's inaccurate self-concept. Hence, client-centered therapists restructure their client's self-concept to correspond better with reality.

According to Rogers, the **process of therapy** is not as important as the **emotional climate** in which it takes place. He believes it is critical for the therapist to provide a supportive emotional climate by

- Being genuine with the client;
- Showing complete, unconditional acceptance of the client as a person; and
- Providing accurate empathy.

In client-centered therapy, the therapist provides relatively little guidance and keeps interpretation and advice to a minimum. The therapist's key task is **clarification**, providing feedback to help clients sort out their feelings and become more comfortable with their genuine selves. (The module includes an excerpt from an actual case.)

Practical Solutions

An article from *Shape* magazine's June 2004 issue, by Angela Hynes, entitled "Reality TV therapy: whether you want a more exciting life, a better career, or more confidence, reality shows can help you achieve your goals," provides an interesting view of reality television as a way to examine our own lives and how we can better ourselves. You can find the article by searching *Shape* magazine with the terms "reality TV therapy" or just put the same phrase into your search engine. Could reality television actually have value beyond entertainment?

11G MODULE

Responding to Stress

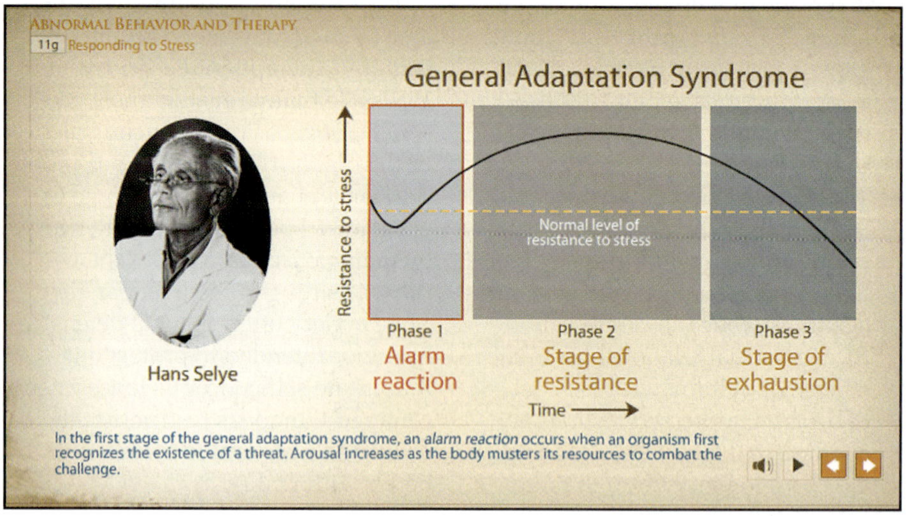

Listen to Hans Selye explain the general adaptation syndrome and our behavioral responses to stress in Module 11g (*Responding to Stress*).

What's It For?

Our response to stress is multidimensional. Stress begins when we make cognitive appraisals that certain events are threatening; this subjective perception of threat typically leads to responses at several levels. Stress often triggers the experience of **emotional responses**, which are often accompanied by **physiological responses**. Stress often leads to **coping efforts**, which represent **behavioral responses**. What stresses you out?

Psychology for a Reason: Responding to Stress

More often than not, stress tends to elicit unpleasant emotions that typically occur along **three dimensions of emotion**, ranging from less to more intense. Typical emotions triggered by stress, listed from least to most intense, include

- Pensiveness, sadness, grief;
- Annoyance, anger, rage; and
- Apprehension, fear, terror.

Strong emotional arousal can sometimes interfere with efforts to cope with stress. According to the **inverted-U hypothesis**, task performance, which is graphed on a vertical axis, should improve with increased emotional arousal—up to a point. After that, further increases in arousal become disruptive, and performance deteriorates. The optimal level of arousal for dealing with stress appears to depend in part on the complexity of the task or the stressful demands. An **intermediate level of arousal** is optimal for tasks of moderate complexity; a **fairly high level of arousal** tends to be optimal for simpler tasks; and a **relatively low level of arousal** tends to be optimal for more complicated tasks. In other words, as a task becomes more complex, the optimal level of arousal tends to decrease.

Emotional responses to stress are often accompanied by **physiological arousal**. **Hans Selye** conducted pioneering research on the effects of prolonged physiological arousal by exposing lab animals to a diverse array of physical and psychological stressors (heat, cold, pain, mild shock, restraint). Based on that research, he formulated the **general adaptation syndrome**, which posits that the body's stress response can move through three stages:

- **Alarm—Phase 1:** A reaction occurs when an organism first recognizes the existence of a threat. Arousal increases as the body musters its resources to combat the challenge.
- **Resistance—Phase 2:** An organism may progress to this phase, during which physiological arousal typically stabilizes at a high level and stress resistance is strong as coping efforts get under way.
- **Exhaustion—Phase 3:** An organism may reach this stage, during which physiological resources are depleted and arousal and stress resistance decline, leading in some cases to exhaustion and physical diseases.

Scientists have since learned more about the details of physiological reactions to stress. There are two major pathways along which the brain sends signals to the **endocrine system** in response to stress. The **hypothalamus** is the brain structure that appears to initiate action along both pathways.

- Action in the **first pathway** begins when signals from the *hypothalamus* are sent to the *pituitary gland*, which secretes the hormone *ACTH*, which in turn stimulates the outer part of the adrenal glands (the *adrenal cortex*) to release **corticosteroids** into the bloodstream. The secretion of corticosteroids leads to increased protein and fat mobilization, increased access to energy storage, and decreased inflammation. Energy is increasing.
- Action in the **second pathway** begins when signals from the *hypothalamus* activate the *sympathetic division of the autonomic nervous system*. A key part of this activation involves stimulating the central part of the adrenal glands (the *adrenal medulla*) to release large amounts of **catecholamines** into the bloodstream. These hormones radiate throughout the body. This secretion of catecholamines leads to increased cardiovascular response, respiration, perspiration, blood flow to active muscles, muscle strength, and mental activity. The body is mobilizing for action.
- Most **behavioral responses** to stress involve **coping**, or efforts to master, reduce, or tolerate the demands created by stress. People cope with stress in many ways. Some are **maladaptive**, relatively unhealthful behavioral efforts to deal with stressful events, whereas others are **constructive**, relatively healthful efforts. PsykTrek offers detailed analyses of these responses.

Practical Solutions

One of the maladaptive ways in which people cope with stress is "indulging oneself," and Internet addiction is an example. The Center for Internet Addiction Recovery provides a website that allows viewers to test whether they are addicted to the Internet (and a study explaining how the test works). To find out if you're addicted to the Internet, go to the Center's homepage (www.netaddiction.com) and find the "Take a test" section. From there, choose "Internet Addiction Test (IAT)" and see how you fare. ■

Conformity and Obedience

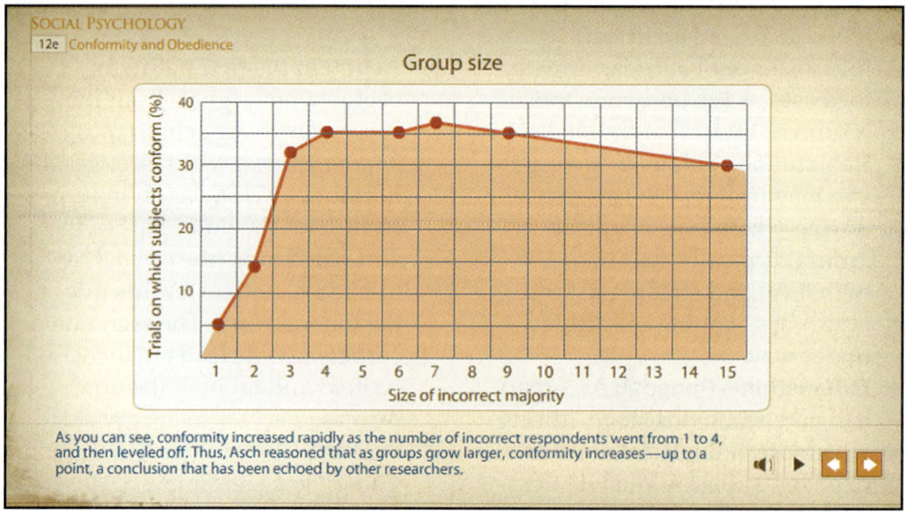

Visit Module 12e (*Conformity and Obedience*) to get more information on Solomon Asch's classic research on conformity.

What's It For?

Does social pressure really influence people? Is "mob mentality" a reality? Do people in groups act differently than they might act alone? What role does authority have in a person's decision-making process? Two classic experiments (one of them quite controversial) were performed to answer these questions.

Psychology for a Reason: Conformity and Obedience

Conformity is defined as yielding to real or imagined social pressure. For example, if you maintain your lawn to keep your neighbors from complaining, you're conforming to social pressure. However, if you do so because you genuinely prefer a nice lawn, that's not conformity.

In the 1950s, **Solomon Asch** devised a classic experiment that reduced ambiguity about whether subjects were conforming. His subjects were male undergraduates recruited for a study of visual perception. A group of seven participants were shown a large card with a vertical line of it and then asked to indicate which of the three lines on a second card matched the original "standard line" in length. All seven subjects were given a turn at the task and announced their choice to the group. However, the person in the sixth chair was the only genuine subject. Everyone else in the group was an accomplice of the experimenter. The accomplices gave accurate responses on the first two trials. On the third trial, line number 2 clearly was the correct response, but the first five "subjects" all said that line number 3 matched the standard line. Over the course of 15 trials, the accomplices all gave the same incorrect response on 12 trials.

The point is this: The line judgments were easy and unambiguous. Only 5% of the control group subjects, who were not exposed to social pressure, made any errors whatsoever over the course of many trials. So when the participants agreed with the accomplices, they weren't making honest mistakes; they were conforming. They were influenced by the accomplices' incorrect answers. The level of conformity varied considerably. Of the 50, 13 never caved in, and 14 conformed on more than half the trials. Averaged across all 50 participants, **conformity** was seen on 37% of the trials. Because the line judgments were clear and very easy, most social scientists viewed the finds as a dramatic demonstration of humans' tendency to conform.

In subsequent studies, Asch found that **group size** and **group unanimity** are key determinants of conformity. Asch's findings indicated that as groups grow larger, conformity increases but only up to a point, a conclusion that has been echoed by other researchers. However, group size made little difference if just one accomplice "broke" with the others, wrecking their unanimous agreement. The presence of another dissenter reduced the number of conforming responses from 37% to 10%. The importance of unanimity in fostering conformity has been replicated in many other studies.

Obedience is defined as following direct commands from someone in authority. Like conformity, obedience is an important form of social influence that social psychologists have studied.

Stanley Milgram conducted classic obedience studies in the 1960s. He was troubled by how readily the citizens of Germany had followed Hitler's orders, even when the orders required morally repugnant actions. His experiment is one of the most famous and controversial studies in psychology.

In his study, the subjects were a diverse collection of 40 men from the local community. They were told they would be participating in a study concerned with the effects of punishment on learning. When they arrived at the lab, they drew slips of paper from a hat to get their assignments. The drawing was rigged so that the subject always became the "teacher" and an accomplice posing as a likable 47-year-old accountant became the "learner." The learner was strapped into an electrified chair through which a shock could be delivered whenever he made a mistake on the task. The subject was then taken to an adjoining room that housed a shock generator that he would control in his role as the teacher. This apparatus had 30 switches designed to administer shocks varying from 15 to 450 volts. Although the apparatus looked and sounded realistic, it was a fake, and the learner was never shocked. (NOTE: PsykTrek includes an extensive collection of footage of Milgram's experiment.)

As the "learning experiment" proceeded, the accomplice made many mistakes that necessitated shocks. The teacher was instructed to increase the shock level after each wrong answer. At 75 volts, the learner began to moan and protest about the shocks. If the participant expressed unwillingness to continue, the experimenter responded with one of four prearranged responses, all delivered sternly, which basically told the participant they had no other choice but to continue. The dependent variable was the maximum shock the participants were willing to administer before refusing to go on. Before the study was conducted, Milgram asked 40 psychiatrists to predict how much shock subjects would be willing to administer. Most predicted fewer than 1% would continue to the end of the series of shocks. However, all the subjects delivered at least 20 levels of shock, and 65% administered all 30 levels, although many displayed considerable distress. Milgram concluded that obedience to authority was even more common than he or others anticipated. Milgram's interpretation of his results led him to argue that commands from an authority figure can make decent people do terribly indecent things. Subsequent studies by Milgram and others showed that females showed as much obedience as males, and obedience rates ran even higher in some other cultures. There were some other variables that affected obedience.

Milgram's critics questioned the ethics of his procedure and noted that subjects were exposed to extensive deception that could undermine their trust in people and to severe stress that could leave emotional scars. But defenders countered that the participants were quickly debriefed and that the short duration of the experiment was worth the astounding findings. Others contended that the results were of questionable generalizability because subjects knew they were taking part in an experiment. They would likely assume that everything must be okay and that they were expected to obey the experimenter's orders. Milgram countered that if subjects thought everything was okay, they would not have experienced distress and that just as subjects may have expected to obey orders from an experimenter, in the real world soldiers and subordinates do the same thing. However, no replications of his obedience study have been conducted in the United States since the mid-1970s.

Practical Solutions

The inspiration for Milgram's study, the actions of those who followed Hitler's orders, is a timeless question. Hitler was not the only person with whom people colluded to commit atrocities, and it is unlikely he will be the last. It is in everyone's best interest to try to understand how conformity and obedience can influence people to act in ways in which they would not act alone. But Milgram's techniques are rightly questionable. Can you think of another way in which Milgram's question can be answered without resorting to ethically questionable experiments?

TO THE OWNER OF THIS BOOK:

I hope that you have found *Psychology,* Enhanced Fifth Edition useful. So that this book can be improved in a future edition, would you take the time to complete this sheet and return it? Thank you.

School and address: ______________________________

____

Department: ______________________________

Instructor's name: ______________________________

1. What I like most about this book is: ______________________________

____

____

2. What I like least about this book is: ______________________________

____

____

3. My general reaction to this book is: ______________________________

____

____

4. The name of the course in which I used this book is: ______________________________

____

5. Were all of the chapters of the book assigned for you to read? ______________________________

   If not, which ones weren't? ______________________________

6. In the space below, or on a separate sheet of paper, please write specific suggestions for improving this book and anything else you'd care to share about your experience in using this book.

____

____

____

____

____

____

____

TAPE HERE.
DO NOT STAPLE.

TAPE HERE.
DO NOT STAPLE.

FOLD HERE

WADSWORTH
CENGAGE Learning™

NO POSTA
NECESSAR
IF MAILE
IN THE
UNITED STA

BUSINESS REPLY MAIL
FIRST-CLASS MAIL PERMIT NO. 34 BELMONT CA

POSTAGE WILL BE PAID BY ADDRESSEE

Attn: Psychology Editor

Wadsworth Cengage Learning
20 Davis Drive
Belmont, CA 94002-9801

FOLD HERE

OPTIONAL:

Your name: ______________________ Date: ____________

May we quote you, either in promotion for *Psychology*, Enhanced Fifth Edition, or in future publishing ventures?

Yes: ____________ No: ____________

Sincerely yours,

James S. Nairne